The Power of a Teacup

A Story of
Art, Love, and
Sacred Gardens

The Power of a Teacup

TEXT AND ILLUSTRATIONS BY

LISSI KAPLAN

Photographs by Amy Neunsinger

 ReganBooks
An Imprint of HarperCollinsPublishers

HarperCollins books may be purchased for educational, business, or sales promotional use. For information please write: Special Markets Department, HarperCollins Publishers Inc., 10 East 53rd Street, New York, NY 10022.

FIRST EDITION

Designed by Cassandra Pappas

Printed on acid-free paper

Library of Congress Cataloging-in-Publication Data

Kaplan, Lissi.
  The power of a teacup : a story of art, love, and sacred gardens / [Lissi Kaplan].—1st ed.
    p. cm.
  ISBN 0-06-008636-X (HC.)
    1. China painting. 2. Art—Psychological aspects.

NK4605 .K278 2002
738.1'5—dc21   2001059035

 03 04 05 06 07 ❖/IM 10 9 8 7 6 5 4 3 2 1

With deep love and gratitude,
I dedicate this book to my husband,
Richard, whose beautiful spirit and tender
heart have touched my soul, and to my
beloved mother, Elaine Gardner Kaplan,
whose beauty and wisdom continue
to inspire me every day

here the spirit does not work
with the hand there is no art.

LEONARDO DA VINCI

Contents

Tea
Time

Acknowledgments

TO MY DAD, Guy Gardner: you're the original artist. And my thanks to Joan and her children for nourishing him so well. I love you all. To my children, Scott, Michelle, and Aaron: I will never stop being amazed by you. My love for you is beyond words and paintings. To my sister Sindi: Thank you for your many talents and wisdom, and for bringing Heather, Marissa, and Ron into my life. They are truly cherished and loved. To my sister Beth: Your courage and love of life are an inspiration, and Lauren and Emily are loved and adored. To my sweet

Aunt Millie, Carrie, and Uncle Jerry: You're dear to my heart. Love and appreciation to my mother- and father-in-law, Willyne and Ira, for bringing Richard into this world, and for your affectionate friendship.

I would like to express my gratitude for all of the love, support, and kindness of Marilyn, Julie, Lauri, Allen, and Linda. It has meant a lot to me. And to my dear friends that bring so much joy and laughter into my life: Leslie, Cathy, Gail, Pam, Debi, Vanessa, Sharon, Nathalie, and Carol. I cherish our friendships.

I wish to thank my publisher, Judith Regan, who saw in me my seeds of possibility. You have my deepest gratitude. Thank you to my editor, Cassie Jones, for your sensitivity to the project. And a special thanks to Mignon McCarthy, for your creative and passionate input.

And, finally, to all of you who now hold this book in your hands: May your gardens always be abundant and fruitful.

The Power of a Teacup

CHAPTER I

"MiMi's Garden"

Everything in nature invites us constantly to
be what we are.   *Gretel Ehrlich*

To talk about teacups and porcelain,
to tell their story and my own, I must
first begin by talking about birds.
My passion for little birds began when I was
nine years old. I grew up on a thirty-acre ranch
in the Great Central Valley of California, a vast
flat patchwork of fields and orchards bordered on

one side by the Sierra Nevada mountains and on the other by the long ribbon of the coast range. My family had orange, grapefruit, and lemon groves and our share of chickens, cows, and horses. On the other side of the coastal mountains were the Monterey Peninsula and the Pacific Ocean.

We had moved to our ranch from the big city of Chicago, where both of my parents were born and raised. My father was a car dealer, like his dad before him, and both of my parents were ready to make a change in their lives, especially my mother. When she was in her early thirties, she became very ill with a rare type of tumor located on her adrenal gland. Here she was with three small children, facing a life-threatening challenge. It became a wish of hers, one to which my dad agreed, that if she survived the surgery and treatment, the whole family would move to a ranch in California and live a peaceful life—a life filled with nature, space, and sunshine. The ranch was also a new adventure for me, because at the time I had only a few friends. Nature and her many creatures became my new playmates.

I would get up early on Saturday mornings and go exploring around the spacious land. I discovered a moist creek bed that ran almost the whole length of our property and was filled with hard-shelled insects, fish scales, and all kinds of interesting rocks.

One time when I was wandering around the creek I noticed a couple of small brown swallows flying under a bridge while others were flying out. Back and forth these cute little birds would go. They seemed so purposeful and dedicated to their task. I was very eager and curious to see just what it was they were so busy doing. So I went under the bridge and found their fascinating work in progress: the swallows were sculpting mud nests on the walls beneath the bridge. I sat there on the muddy bank of the creek for at least an hour, amazed at how disciplined and devoted they were in building the beautiful, smooth, cocoon-shaped birdhouses. I remember at the time wishing that I could be a little bird so I could experience being part of such a cozy, safe environment. Birds always seemed so happy to me.

One Saturday as I was leaving the bridge I noticed an injured swallow on the ground, struggling to fly. I ran home and got my bicycle, quickly lining my basket with a towel and packing a small thermos of sugar water and an eyedropper, and I rushed back to rescue the injured bird. This became my Saturday-morning ritual,

and I always found one or two—a swallow, a finch, a wren—hidden behind bushes or lying beneath a tree.

I would cup the tiny birds in my small hands and, as gently as I could manage, place these wounded flyers in my basket and feed them droplets of sugar water. Then I would ride home with my feathered patients. I always kept a small shoebox waiting on a wooden picnic table in our backyard. Sometimes it would require a couple of days of box rest and lots of verbal encouragement for them to become strong enough that I could gently lift them up into the air, wish them well, and happily set them free, hoping that I would see them again one day.

THIS GIRLHOOD MEMORY was brought back to me several years ago when my mother was dying and it became time to say good-bye. During those months, I would bring her biscuits—she liked Cadbury's shortbread—and make her tea. We used her beautiful antique cups. She could manage only herbal tea, so we drank soothing, warm chamomile together, sitting side by side on her sofa. Very slowly, my mother would

close her eyes, breathe in the fragrance of the tea, and take a sip. She would tap lightly on her saucer as if drawn to an inner beat, or to the bell-like sound that only porcelain can make.

I savored the tea and the time with her. On some visits, we just sat quietly together for several hours. She seemed to like that. Other times, we talked of many things. We talked about our memories of the ranch—the smell of orange blossoms in the spring, and the smell of brownies baking in the afternoon in any season. We talked about her dying. One afternoon shortly before she died we shared a sacred moment.

She was lying in her bed, and I sat next to her as we spoke. Her room was decorated in soft shades of peach and French blue. Her comforter was embellished with hand-stitched roses and vines. She had a beautiful vanity, with all her cosmetics neatly lined up next to exotic perfume bottles and a mirror that always seemed to be illuminated. I remember as a young girl how much I loved sitting on her silk stool in front of that vanity, trying on all of her makeup and wishing that one day I would look like her. I loved the way she wore her colored eye shadow—iridescent greens and lavenders were her favorites. She still managed to put a little makeup on each morning, even though she had become frail and weak.

We both felt very peaceful that day. I held her hand and said, "Mom, close your eyes and try to remember one of the happiest moments in your life—a moment when you felt pure joy."  She closed her eyes and exhaled softly. After a little bit, she said, "My happiest time—besides having my three daughters, of course—was when I was about twelve years old in Chicago. I was ice-skating around and around on an outdoor rink. My arms were outstretched, and I was gliding on the smooth, silky ice with the wind against my cheeks and my hair blowing in the chilly air. I felt so free; free as a bird." Then she paused and said softly, like a secret, "I'm coming back, you know. I'm coming back as a hummingbird. You'll know me when you see me. I'll always be watching over you and your sisters. You'll see."

My mother, whom we called MiMi, was a lyric soprano and master voice teacher. She used to open the back door at home so that she could drink in the vistas of the mountains while she sang. Birds chirped right along with her—in perfect harmony, it seemed to me.

She had her own unique relationship with birds. She used to say that birds are very spiritual creatures: "They are God's messengers. Look at

their eyes, they are so wise, so deep." She especially loved the exquisite beauty of humming-
birds, and it made perfect sense to me that she
chose the hummingbird as her alter ego. My
mother had red hair and startling emerald eyes,
and to gentle her vocal cords, she wore brightly
colored scarves around her neck, just like an iridescent hummingbird's ruby and sapphire gorge,
the delicate feathered throat.

A FEW MONTHS AFTER my mother died, I
wandered through her house. The china cabinets
were still full. Antique silver and pieces of hand-
painted porcelain had a place in every room.
These beautiful porcelains were part of the interior landscape of our house, the embroidered

background of my childhood. My mother liked to use her fine china for every special family occasion. She decorated the table lavishly with her rust-colored, hand-painted china from Hungary. She had everything from crescent-shaped salad bowls to covered soup bowls with hand-carved porcelain roses on top. She would spend days preparing the table with her finest ecru linens and Venetian glass goblets that had gold-fish hand-blown on the bottom of each stem. The room would glow like a warm amber flame.

Her porcelains were her passion. She loved collecting teacups and pots from different countries she visited. I wanted to relive those joyful family celebrations. I longed to hear my mother play the piano and sing all her favorite show tunes just one more time, but it was not meant to be. I knew that I would have to try to re-create

that happiness in my own life now. That day I picked up one precious piece after another. I felt a deep sense of warmth as I thought of the moments spent with my mother over tea. I found myself really looking at this china, seeing it as if for the first time. Some of the pieces were more than a century old. In her will, my mother had left me many pieces, among them a cream-and-gold English porcelain serving bowl made in 1891, with a leaf cut-motif rim and wild roses painted wistfully around the inside. The bowl hasn't a single chip after all those many years.

I caressed the teacups, the plates, the bowls, and thought to myself, Somebody painted this cup, this plate, this bowl more than a hundred years ago. I felt as if I were peering into the deep past, connecting to an artist of long ago whose brush had touched the piece of porcelain that I now held in my hands. The connection to the past and to the art form was immediate and powerful in a way that defies explanation. I felt as if the porcelain were speaking directly to a place deep inside me. Normally restless, I stood still there in my mother's house for what seemed like hours, studying her porcelain. I felt a particular excitement at the same time. I thought, Who's painting these pieces now?

I have been obsessed with this art form ever since.

When I got home I sealed myself up in the first-floor guest room of our house. I emptied it out and created my first studio. Nothing mattered but learning everything I could about porcelain, and about painting on porcelain. I felt an immense wave of energy carrying me. At the time I thought I was learning only about this extraordinary art form. I didn't know then that this complete absorption was to take me to places I'd never been before, places inside myself.

I used to notice other artists—painters, sculptors, musicians—losing themselves in their craft, tapping the source, it seemed to me. I longed for the direct experience of that self-forgetting. It seemed out of reach to me for so many years. In my first marriage, I raised three beautiful children, but my relationship with my husband spun out of control, and my heart was broken. It was so hard during those days to be still, to be in the moment, to be myself. For many years, as a result of that trauma, I felt so lost inside. I needed to find my own sense of peace within myself to begin to heal, but I didn't know how to reach that place. It became very clear to me that if I didn't break away from my marriage,

I would never find the life that I so prayed to have. It was extremely difficult for me to push through all that pain, but I knew I had to find my happiness. I believe it is out there for all who seek it—and I was on my path, my own unique heart path toward healing.

When I allowed myself to follow this inexplicable and humble passion to learn to paint on porcelain, there it was, as though it had been waiting for me, as if it had always been there. The source, the creative well, the coming home. The feeling of connecting to that still point in the center.

Porcelain is my canvas now. I spend each day painting on its smooth, white, satin surface.

That first year I created a porcelain flower garden for my mother's hummingbird, who was a frequent visitor to my backyard. I painted a symphony of floating French flowers from my imagination in yellows, pinks, and blues on an entire collection of porcelain, including tea sets, vases, plates, bowls, and candlesticks. It was to honor my mother and reflect her joyful spirit. I called it "MiMi's Garden."

This was my first collection, the first set of pieces I felt ready to show outside the cloister of my studio. Since then, I have created many porcelain gardens—the whimsical, fanciful, and romantic gardens of my imagination—for family, for friends, for people I am meeting for the first time.

I BELIEVE WE ALL have a garden inside us, a garden of many colors and shapes that needs to be watered and nurtured and loved. The seeds of the garden are the possibilities and passions that are deep within and that need to open in order to take root and flourish and thrive. When I'm painting a garden for someone, I first look to see those seeds of possibility in the person. The seeds are always there. I then create a garden uniquely in that person's essence, as I did for my mother.

My own seeds were always there too, but they were buried and neglected for many years. I had to look at them and love them and trust that higher voice from inside of me that kept saying, "Use all I have given you, see the gifts and the seeds that have been waiting to be noticed, waiting to be loved. The garden you grow will be beautiful, because it's your own unique garden." I now believe that I have the ability to pass that gift on to my clients through my eyes, through my heart, to my hands, and there is pure joy in showing someone how beautiful they are in the reflection of their own unique porcelain garden.

When I paint, I get quiet and enter the heart of silence. I hold a bowl or cup in my left palm as I paint it, and I feel as if I'm holding the whole universe in my hand. When I present a finished piece to someone, it feels like an offering. I think of what must have been the first teacup, a simple handleless diminutive bowl, shaped and fired by a master potter in China thousands of years ago. The connection is ancient, and I feel it strongly. I've learned that even a teacup can lead you to yourself.

People ask me, "How did you choose porcelain?"

I offer this answer: "I didn't choose porcelain. I never set out to be a porcelain artist. Porcelain chose me."

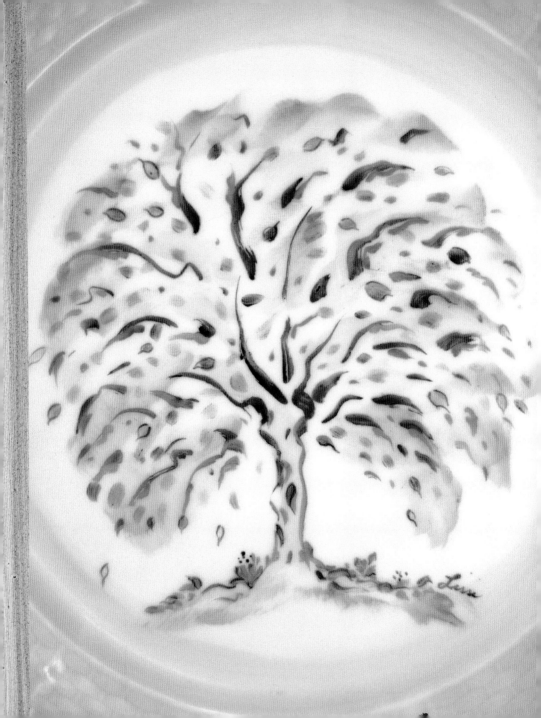

CHAPTER 2

Ancient Rituals

To forget one's ancestors is to be a brook
without a source, a tree without a root.

Chinese proverb

Early in the morning, when the sun
has cast its golden glow, I head
downstairs to the studio. The light
is already streaming through the big south win-
dows that face out to the garden in the backyard.
It's there that all my familiar trees, flowers, and

rose and hibiscus bushes are waiting for me to glance their way as I paint and feel their essence throughout my day.

On my worktable are my vials of paint, glass palette, palette knife, and oils of lavender and clove. Their intoxicating fragrance fills the house as if some ancient incense is burning, calling me to it each day.

The glass palette that always sits in the center of my worktable is already clean this morning. When I've finished painting one collection and am ready to begin another, I prefer to clean the palette. Some porcelain artists like to save their paints from project to project; I discard mine. The process of cleaning and discarding is a ritual of completion for me. It empties the palette and opens my imagination for the next collection to come in.

My brushes, handmade out of sable and squirrel, work hard for me, and like my paints come from all over the world. I have four favorite brushes, and I handle them very carefully; I want them to last. It can take months to work in a brush to render it pliable and responsive to my particular stroke. When the brushes are well-oiled and soft, they pick up the paint like a sponge picks up water, and the strokes of paint are translucent and smooth, which gives the porcelain painting its special soft and dreamy effect.

The porcelain artist is part mineralogist and part alchemist. The paints are powdered metallic oxides that I mix with oil of lavender and oil of cloves. The powdered pigments used on porcelain are different from those used by other types of artists because in the hot fire of the kiln they melt into porcelain like water into sand and become one with it. I keep a journal of the color recipes I have created.

My kiln, the porcelain artist's oven, looks kind of like a brick igloo. It has a lid on top with a peephole so that I can check to see if the fire is on or off. The temperature inside the kiln can reach as high as 2,200 degrees Fahrenheit. When my pieces are ready for their final fire, I have a little ritual I like to do for good luck. After I have carefully placed the pieces in the kiln and am ready to close the lid and begin the fire, I say affectionately to the painted porcelains, "Okay, ladies, you look beautiful! Make me proud, ladies! I'll see you in the morning. Good night." While I'm asleep, the paints, the porcelain, and the intense heat in the kiln create their magical union, and I always look forward to that hot gush of air in my morning face as I unload the new treasures. The sheer beauty of color melted into creamy white porcelain never fails to take my breath away.

THE CHINESE CREATED the formula for making porcelain in A.D. 1400, and eventually the ancient technique made its way to different parts of the world. Deep beds of china clay were later found in Europe along seams running under Germany and France and in a vast field in southwest England—clay as pure and primordial as that found in China thousands of years earlier. China clay is the purest of all clays, a descendant of the great rocks of the earth. It took the earth hundreds of millions of years to produce it. When I'm working and holding the porcelain piece in my hand, I'm keenly aware of the ancient connection that predates the existence of flowers on our planet. It's very powerful to me.

One of the tools I use every day and am quite fond of is a wooden-handled palette knife that dates back to 1915. The palette knife and a number of other porcelain-painting tools and supplies were given to me as a gift. One afternoon the mother of a friend and client of mine came over because she wanted to buy her daughter Pam a birthday gift. I had painted a special design for Pam about a year earlier called "Pam's Garden."

We walked around the studio for a while looking at all the different shapes of porcelain pieces and then finally decided on a beautiful chocolate pot that we thought Pam would love. Then, with a twinkle in her eye, she said, "I have something that belongs to you in my car. I'll be right back." I was puzzled. Moments later she came back hold-

ing a cardboard box that was neatly wrapped in plastic, protecting the contents. "This is for you," she said. "It's been waiting for you."

Pam's mother had given me the gift of someone's treasured porcelain painting tools, paints, and a small wooden box that held many more intricate tools, all in pristine condition. The faint fragrance of the lavender and clove oils had become part of the box.

While on vacation in rural Pennsylvania several years earlier, she stopped at a small antique store along the road and became attracted to the collection of porcelain-painting tools that were on display, although she was not a porcelain painter. When she returned home, she put them away and didn't use them. She said that when she met me, she knew I would cherish them.

The box contained a postmarked letter that

ultimately enabled my husband, Richard, an art dealer experienced in art research, to trace these priceless tools back to their original owner, a woman born sometime around the turn of the last century. Her name was Henrietta Jordan, and she was a schoolteacher and amateur china painter in Pennsylvania. Using her mahogany-handled palette knife every day connects me to her. Sometimes I say out loud while mixing my paints with her knife, "Let's paint something beautiful today, Henrietta. We'll do it together."

CHAPTER 3

Sacred Gardens

Come along inside. . . . we'll see if tea and
buns can make the world a better place.

The Wind in the Willows

Nature is now my teacher, my laboratory, my muse.

This wasn't always so. For much
of my adult life I was too busy, distracted, and
frantic inside to notice more than if the sky was
blue or not. When I was in my thirties and the

youngest of my three children was five, I wanted to get ready for the next stage in my life, so I enrolled in a three-year interior design program. While working on assignments that required studying and illustrating landscapes, architecture, and still-life forms, I slowly began to tap into the joy and wonder of that little girl from long ago who lived on a ranch, the girl who loved to explore and be surrounded by nature. Design school began to really open up my mind and heart to new possibilities. It prepared me to be a

porcelain artist because it opened my eyes to see what was before me in a way with which I had lost touch.

Now, in this stage of life, all things are alive to me—the intricate petals of a flower or even the intricacy of a stamen can hold me captive. I study their natural form, their uniqueness, and their great beauty, and they move me. I feel as if I'm able to see them in a way that wasn't available to me until now.

I also have to be able to see the person for whom I'm creating a porcelain garden. When a client or friend makes an appointment to come for a personal garden sitting, we first begin in my kitchen, where there is lots of natural light and a table set with a simple white linen cloth and napkins and the aroma of freshly baked scones, which I serve with fresh clotted cream and jam.

There's nothing quite like the simple joy of tea, a good scone, and pleasant conversation. My kitchen is filled with little vignettes of many different porcelains that I have painted over the years. Large blossoms on top of tall stalks of rose and hibiscus bushes peer in at us from outside the window.

Soon the conversation becomes a bit more intimate and reflective. Perhaps it is because of the ritual of the tea itself; charming hand-painted cups and saucers, dainty little stirring spoons, sugar bowls, and small individual teapots conjure up memories of tea parties with imaginary or real guests from our long-ago childhoods. The client and I simply enjoy the moment, sipping tea and watching the flickering of a scented candle, and the conversation flows quite naturally.

Before we know it, a few hours have passed,

and we have each shared stories of great moments and great losses, passions and hobbies, disappointments and victories, desires and dreams. Sometimes I get so absorbed in their stories that I take all their feelings and emotions and store them inside for a while. Eventually I'm able to express in artistic form their own unique inner garden, a garden that will become an heirloom to be passed on from generation to generation to honor their life and the life of their loved ones.

I can remember my mother saying when I was a girl, "I'm getting the tea and biscuits ready, Lissi. Come, let's talk." Now I get to create that special feeling when someone comes to my home for tea and we share a moment, a memory, but mostly a feeling—a feeling that when they enter my haven they feel a combination of love and acceptance over a warm, sweet cup of tea.

I've been given the honor of painting heirlooms for family and friends, and for people I'm meeting for the first time. They will be passed on like a legacy from mother to daughter, sister to sister, aunt to niece, wife to husband, sister to brother, grandparent to grandchild, friend to friend, and on and on like a colorful tapestry woven together celebrating and bonding us for generations to come. They are like perfect little pearls, each with its own rare beauty, forming a rich and elegant necklace. There is power in a teacup, for it contains endless memories and cherished moments. If you look carefully at each brush stroke, you will see an intimate portrait of a life lived in all its many colors and textures.

I'M TOLD THAT MY great-great-grandmother Sarah on my mother's side was a well-known healer in Poland. They say that people would come from great distances and line a path to her home so that they could feel her healing hands cupped around their broken bodies and injured souls. At times I feel as though she's working with me when I paint my sacred, healing gardens.

When I was very young, my mother discovered that I was intuitively able to find an area in her back that was the source of an occasional pinched nerve. I can remember visualizing and then tracing with my fingers the veins on my mother's temple to her neck, then moving my hands over her shoulder toward the middle of her back. I would begin gently kneading in a circular motion and then apply more pressure with my little fingers until my mother let out a huge

sigh of relief. "You did it!" she said, and that's when she shared with me the story of her great-grandmother, Sarah the healer, and how I had inherited her healing hands. My father began to seek my expertise in eliminating the occasional shooting pains he was prone to in his legs; a foot massage solved the problem.

I don't know if my great-great-grandmother Sarah ever painted, but I believe that she has helped me with a stroke or two from time to time. Learning about the ancient art form of porcelain painting has given me the profound gift of being

able to touch and be touched. I have been privi-
leged to paint many sacred gardens, and I have
come to love them as my own.

Every night when I am done working, I massage my hands lovingly with cream, and I kiss
them and thank them for their gifts of service.
My hands have helped to set me free.

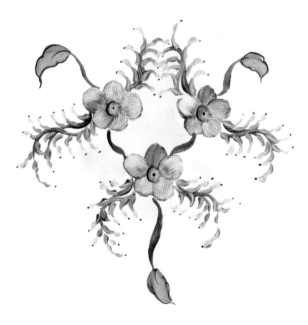

CHAPTER 4

The Rose

It's not the hand alone that does the writing,
the painting, but the whole being.

Kitaoji Rosanjin

I remember picking up the porcelain brushes for the first time. I had painted with oils and with watercolors on canvas and on paper, but I had never painted on porcelain before. Its smooth, slippery surface makes porcelain painting one of the most difficult art forms there is. One piece might go through six firings, and once fixed by fire the paint will not fade, and is permanent, invulnerable to the ravages of time.

When I started painting I had no real master teacher or mentor. I had taken a few beginner classes locally, but I more or less learned this art form on my own, studying antiques and reading every porcelain book I could get my hands on. I practiced eight to ten hours a day every day for several months. There were times when I painted for so many hours that my fingers blistered. I couldn't understand why this art was so difficult.

I realize now that the real reason for my tremendous drive to succeed in learning porcelain painting had a lot to do with my own fears and heartbreak. Being exposed to illness, sadness, and death for long periods of time can change a

person. It can either slow you down or help push you through to a much deeper level of understanding of just how precious and valuable life really is. A thought kept going through my mind: "No more waiting."

Several years ago my younger sister had very aggressive breast cancer. Then, six months after she completed her final stem cell transplant, my mother was diagnosed with a severe case of breast cancer. My sister, thank God, has survived and is in remission, and after my mother lost her brave two-year battle with cancer I found that my way of dealing with the pain of losing her was to paint. Every stroke I painted helped me grieve for her. Every petal I tried to paint was a peeling of the many layers of our lives together, all the lessons that she taught me, lessons that continue to stay with me.

One lesson I'll always cherish is the gift she gave me of being myself. To just be. When I was young, if she saw my sisters or me just daydreaming in our rooms, looking out of the window, or staring at the ceiling, she would never say, "What are you doing? What are you thinking? Is your homework done?" She understood that everyone needs a little idle time to figure things out or just to daydream a bit. I remember she once said that nobody's blank inside. With a little idle time, our subconscious mind opens up, and powerful things can come in. So she would just let us be—so that we could have the freedom to think and imagine, so that we could be who we are. This was an enormous gift from her to us. I've found my way back to that place now as an adult, and I'm deeply grateful.

Sometimes during the middle of the afternoon after I've been painting for several hours, I go out in the yard and lay in the soft grass. I rest my eyes, I rest my hands, I rest my mind, and just let go. This allows me a chance to reconnect to myself and to nature, and to feel my mother's presence. Occasionally when I least expect it my mother's hummingbird will come into the yard, rest her sweet body on a branch, and sing to me as I'm lying on the grass looking up. I'll smile, and with a tear in my eye I'll say, "Hi, Mom, you look beautiful. I miss you."

Once while I was lying on the grass my mother's hummingbird surprised me with a gift. She dropped one of her feathers from the sky and it floated down slowly, landing on my face. It felt like her soft kiss. I was so touched by the sweetness of that moment, I held the precious little feather and caressed it with tenderness. I keep it wrapped in a soft handkerchief and carry it with me wherever I go. I know this was her way of saying, "I'm watching you, and I love you always."

You have to be in a very peaceful place in your life to be a porcelain artist. You need to have a reverence for quiet and the capacity for complete focus and attention on the subject before you. The art form also demands enormous patience and the willingness to cultivate that quality. Having found true love with my husband, Richard, three years after my divorce gave me that peace. Richard, like my mother, lets me be free with his unconditional love and complete understanding of my true nature. With him by my side I can freely give from my soul to myself, to my loved ones, and to this art form.

My real challenge in porcelain painting was learning to paint the rose, the most complex and complicated of all flowers. Painting the rose is the Mount Everest that every porcelain artist must climb. If you can master the rose, you can paint any flower—that's how crucial the technique is to learn. I knew in my heart that if I could master the rose it would set me free.

I began to learn slowly by studying roses in my backyard. For weeks I carefully examined each petal, each stamen, each stem, each leaf. I looked at the layering pattern of the petals, which grow one over the other, gracefully overlapping to form a whole flower, each petal connected to one another and all touching the core, the heart at the center of the flower. I practiced painting my first roses on a porcelain tile, but to my great frustration and disappointment the roses came out looking stiff, flat, and lifeless, even though I had been practicing them every day for hours at a time. This impasse went on for more than a month, constantly challenging my will and determination and frustrating me to the point of tears more than once. But it never occurred to me to quit or give up.

Then, late one evening, it happened. I made the breakthrough! I tried to lift the petals of the rose off the porcelain tile with my brush—to somehow pull out the texture and bring it to dimensional life. It was in that upward stroking with my brush and the slight twisting movement with my wrist that I was able to tease out the color and form the curled edge effect on the

Lissi's first rose

tips of the petals. That night I went to bed with my brush in hand, practicing like an orchestra conductor. Richard thought I was losing my mind.

THE NEXT MORNING I realized that I had to go my own way with my painting technique, just as I had done years ago with my singing. From age thirteen into my twenties, I studied voice, ultimately training for opera at a school that prepares its students for New York City's Metropolitan Opera. I was gifted with a coloratura soprano voice, and I liked to swoop my notes and sing the entire range. I like to do the same now in my painting. I know now that it's my nature to do so, to launch myself forward, to trust the voice, the imagination. Singing taught me discipline and prepared me to be a porcelain artist.

The day I finally painted my first real rose—one of which I could be proud—I felt as though I had accomplished something powerful. I stood back and admired the finished cream-colored flower with its yellow-brown heart and its many layers of petals, and I cried. The vase that bears that rose sits proudly on the fireplace mantel in my bedroom, and I see it each morning and night. Just looking at it inspires me and encourages me to never be afraid of facing adversity in my life.

I will always look at a rose with deep appreciation and love. The rose was my teacher, my friend, my healer. Petal by petal, layer by layer, I have healed my heart, found my happiness, and found my place. The rose has set me free, and I will be eternally grateful.

CHAPTER 5

Free As a Bird

The shell must break before the bird can fly.

Alfred, Lord Tennyson

I saw a little brown swallow today as I was walking on a trail in the foothills near my home. It came to rest upon a branch as I stood still, hoping it would stay for a while. After a moment, I said in a whisper, "I want to thank you for all of the life lessons you have taught me. You were right about living a life with purpose, dedication, and a measure of discipline, and to remember that we should always celebrate each day with a song." Lifting a small twig from the branch, the cute little visitor then took flight and soon was out of sight. I smiled to think of the cozy little mud nest it was building—with one more twig on the way.

As I continued along the path I came upon my favorite wild rose bush, which must have been born from a seed carried on nature's breath to this beautiful place. I sat for a moment and held a fallen petal. I closed my eyes and felt the rose's velvet coolness on my face. I inhaled its sweet perfume, enjoying its essence.

Occasionally, I'm caught by the thought that I'm squandering away my time in these occupations, that I'm wasting my day. But I'm caught less and less by this thinking. With gratitude, I get to be an interpreter of the natural world—through my eyes, to my heart, then to my hands—for the pure joy of it.

When I paint a teacup or another piece of porcelain, I hold it in my hands from start to finish. I am the only one who has touched that piece. There's a kind of power in this, and I know it will be felt by whoever comes to own that cup or that entire collection. And knowing this, in turn, inspires me as I paint. When I began working with porcelain, I could feel that my heart was coming along for the ride. This journey has changed my life. It continues to do so every day.

As I headed home for my own cozy mud nest, I felt a strong sense of contentment. I pictured my mother ice-skating again with the wind in her hair and her bright smile and took comfort in the

fact that wherever she was at that moment, she was feeling free as a bird. I stopped for a moment and opened my mother's handkerchief that holds her tiny feather, I looked up at the heavens and said, Thank you.

Come enter your heart of silence . . . be still.

Can you hear?

Can you see?

Can you feel?

Do you see what I see? I see you . . .

in all your beauty. . . .

I can see your seeds of possibilities,

seeds of hope, seeds of dreams. . . .

It's time to nourish them with love and

encouragement and let them grow and

live the life they were meant to live. . . .

You have inside you a sacred garden.

LISSI KAPLAN